Healthy Habits Every Day

How To Change Your Lifestyle In 21 Days

Anne Gilmore

<u>Table of Contents</u>

Introduction

Have you ever sat down and pondered over some questions that are focused on your habits? I am confident that this is a question we have all asked ourselves at one time or another. I know that I personally have asked this question when I wanted to know why I couldn't learn to use my body differently overnight, why I couldn't maintain better eating habits past the second week of trying, or why I couldn't maintain, over time, my new habit of believing that I am enough just as I am.

You need to understand that creating habits is exactly like learning to meditate. When we practice meditating, we often hear practitioners refer to our wandering thoughts as a dog that wanders away. The same is true for our minds when we meditate. When people meditate, they focus on something: a candle, a word or phrase, or their breath, noting its inhalations and exhalations. Often our mind will wander and begin thinking random thoughts, such as, "I need to get milk at the grocery store," or "I wonder what I should wear today." Meditators are typically taught to watch their thoughts as a neutral witness; say to themselves, "There has been thinking"; and then return to concentrating on the defined target of focus. For most people, this is an arduous practice, as it was for me this morning. My mind just kept wandering away like a very curious dog. I kept reining it in, but it kept wandering away. So, that became my practice - the practice of returning to my point of focus.

Learning a new habit is exactly the same. You will tumble over obstacles and go back to the old behaviors or habits several times. Why does this happen? What can we do to work past these old behaviors so as to create new, healthy habits?

Initiating and implementing new, healthy habits requires slowing down and becoming self-aware. It also requires a ton of practice, regularity and a heap of self-kindness for those times when we do wander and go back to our old habits! That's bound to happen, so instead of beating yourself up for eating those two pieces of pie and tons of holiday cookies, give yourself a break. Notice what you ate, be compassionate with yourself and gently return to where you want your focus to be. It is not enough to want to do something differently. It's important to realize that we have been employing other habits of behavior for a very long time. So, be sure to add a truckload of self-awareness, a bottomless pit of self-compassion and a relentless dedication to the regular practice of your new, healthy habits.

I would love to give you some simple steps to make new healthy habits part of your typical routine, but I would be lying to say that changing yourself is easy. Changing ourselves for the better is one of the most courageous things we can do. So, be kind to yourself. Treat yourself like you would treat someone you love as you attempt the courageous act of creating new, healthy habits for yourself!

Chapter 1: First Phase

Day 1: Note Down Your Goals

I cannot stress enough how important it is to not only have goals, but to write them down. To me, if it is not written down it is merely a wish or a dream. A written goal has legitimacy and a purpose that dreams just do not. Writing down your goals will help you to remember them in vivid detail, especially when the road gets tougher. Remember, a goal recognizes you are not currently where you want to be, but provides recognition that you do have the desire and the ability to find a path to get there.

Take 5 minutes or 60 minutes, whatever it takes, and write down 3-5 goals that you hope to accomplish in this process. Write down 3-5 goals that you want to achieve in the next 21 days, two months or one year to come. Finally, write out 3-5 crazy, out-of-this-world goals that you're almost too embarrassed to admit. I'll share with you one of mine. I am not in the entertainment business. I am not an actor, I am not a director, nor do I have a talent for either of these things. However, I have a goal to win an Oscar and stand on that stage by the time I'm 45 years old. I know it's crazy, but it's on my list…see, it's not so hard. The important thing is to HAVE goals, no matter how "out there" they are. If you do not have a clear view of where you are going, how are you ever going to get there?

If you're still having trouble coming up with your goals, then try answering these questions:

1. What do I want to get out of this book?
2. What vacation would I love to take with my family?
3. How much money do I want to make?

If the above questions don't get you where you feel like you need to be, it's ok to start a little broader. For example, "What does a better me look

7

like?"

Now that your goals have been articulated AND written down, spend the day thinking about them. Make sure they are important to you and on the path towards where you ultimately want to go. From personal experience, achieving a goal that has little to no true meaning to you will be extremely difficult.

Have an awesome day and let's meet up again tomorrow after you have let your goals percolate a bit!

Day 2: Determine a Reason to be Optimistic Today

First, always be optimistic: You might have observed some people in your life who never consider taking a positive approach to their lives, rather they keep obsessing about past regrets. They always focus on the negative prior incidents, rather than the positive experiences they have encountered. So, they need to shift to an optimistic approach to life that can help them understand how to stay happy throughout their life.

Pause and ponder about this for a moment. We are always searching for evidence to confirm the worst. I won't get that job because I am too old or too young. I will never win because I never win anything. I can't afford a new car, new dress or a new coat. So we don't get the job, win the contest or buy that new thing. We don't even try. If you don't enter a contest, you certainly cannot win it.

We don't try because we already know the reason why something won't work for us, so it becomes a self-fulfilling prophecy. What would happen if we looked for a reason why something positive will happen instead? Our attitude about trying would change for the better. That's the first thing that will happen – we start off with a positive attitude and march forward.

Take this moment to imagine one reason why you will accomplish the goal you want to succeed at today. If you can find two, make a mental note of two. When you find three reasons why something will work for you instead of fail, you are well on your way.

Now look for the evidence you are right to believe you will accomplish this goal. Be open to little things such as encouraging words from people, a chance meeting or an unexpected stroke of luck. The more you look, the more you will find. Give thanks for each piece of evidence and accept it with a grateful heart.

Here's a powerful way to reinforce your desire to succeed at anything today. Say out loud, "I am optimistic. I know good things are happening for me. Thank you. Thank you. Thank you."

Repeat it throughout the day – especially if you find nagging doubt about something you want to do. Say it. Think it. Be it. Find a reason to be optimistic. Remember, there is always a reason, so dig as deep as necessary in order to surface it.

Day 3: Make or Organize Your Bed

Before you leave the house this morning, make your bed. I know it seems like a small and trivial task, but I have a feeling it will work wonders for you. It is a task that only requires a few minutes of your time but can help jumpstart your day in ways you have probably never dreamed imaginable. Key benefits include:

- Starting your day with productivity

Starting out with something productive will help you maintain that mindset as you face more difficult challenges throughout your day.

- Starting your day with something active

Get up, get moving and get the blood flowing to activate the awesomeness coming your way today.

- Starting your day by checking something off your list

Completing a task can set off a chain reaction of activities designed at completing more tasks. Start with something small and work your way up to something HUGE!

- Starting your day with a WIN

It is always a positive when you start out your day with a goal and then you achieve it; no matter how small that goal may be.

In addition to the many benefits making your bed has on the start of your day, it can be beneficial to the end of your day as well. A made bed is considerably more appealing to crawl into after you've just crushed your day. And, with any luck, the appealing bed you so diligently made earlier this morning will produce a better night's rest to help you move even closer to your goals tomorrow.

Already make your bed every day? Spend time reflecting on how it is a positive in your life that is helping you achieve your goals. I'd be willing to bet, you've never thought about this daily routine as something that will drive you closer to your dream life. Want extra credit? Write yourself a positive note and leave it on your pillow as a gift to yourself for the end of the day.

Day 4: Be Grateful for Everything

We often think of happiness as causing us to spontaneously jump up and down for joy, laugh hysterically or smile until our cheeks burst.

Of course, those are all outward signs of happiness.

But you don't always have to make a spectacle of yourself to be happy.

Sometimes you can just be still and content, enjoying the feeling that everything is all right.

Remember being a kid and laying on the grass just gazing at the sky? At that moment, everything was all right in the world. Sure, there were bad things going on in the world. But you didn't care at that moment in time, just laying there gazing at the sky. To you, everything was all right. And so that's how you let everything be in that singular, magical moment.

That's being grateful. That's happiness too.

How wonderful life is when we can be grateful for nothing at all. Little kids have this ability down pat.

You were a little kid once. You shook off the worries of the day and just gazed at the sky. Now the ups and downs of the years have taken their toll. It's not so easy anymore.

Or is it?

That little sky gazing kid is still you. Now is a good time to let your inner kid out again and be grateful for seemingly nothing at all.

Take a few minutes to remember a sky gazing moment. Maybe you were mesmerized by the ocean. Maybe you lost yourself in a blade of grass. Maybe you were caught in the magic of falling snow.

Search your heart and find that memory. Bring it forward and feel it all over again. Then go outside. Lose yourself in the sky, the moon, the stars, the rain, or whatever catches your fancy.

Be still and just let everything be right with the world again.

Try this affirmation, "I am young in spirit and free. I see the good in life and good comes to me. I am blessed with a wonderful, warm home. I am blessed with *[insert two of your most readily apparent positive aspects of your life]."*

Day 5: Mark Your Nutrition

Today's activity involves writing down everything that goes into your body. I would like for you to keep a food journal that tracks your food and beverage intake for an entire day. The idea here is to not beat yourself up for the food choices that you're making, but to have an inventory of what you are consuming. Knowledge is power, especially with your food.

We all know that your body needs fuel, but we also know that it needs the right type. We are operating high-performance machines! You probably wouldn't put the lowest grade of gas into a Lamborghini, would you? Why do the same to your body? You also wouldn't keep pumping after the tank is full, right? So, no need to keep eating once your body tells you it's had enough.

I feel that most of us (myself definitely included) do not realize how much we are eating in a given day or how often. Snacking, when not controlled, can be a dangerous increase in calories. In addition to how often we are eating, most of us struggle with portion control. The hope is that by keeping a log of food and beverage intake then we can make better choices going forward leading to improved health, energy and stamina.

If you need help tracking, it can be as simple as a piece of paper or as extensive as a notebook purchased strictly for this exercise. Another great option would be an app. Numerous free apps are available that help you track your food and beverage intake and can make it very simple and convenient for you. The idea here is to make it as simple as possible so that you are able to stick with it.

Oh, and one last thing, DO NOT READ YOUR JOURNAL. We will work on the results tomorrow, but for tonight, only write and track; do not read.

Day 6: Smile Before Leaving the House

We put on shirts, skirts or pants, and shoes. We pick our colors in all kinds of hues. We dress to express and impress.

We wear boots to protect against the snow. We wear coats to protect against the rain. We wear hats to protect against the sun.

We slip on sunglasses and sandals. We carry purses and bags. We grab laptops, cell phones and keys.

We arm ourselves with all the tools we need to face the day. Except we forget the one fashion accessory we really need – a smile.

Smiles can open closed minds and melt warm hearts. They can turn a 'no' into a 'yes' in the blink of an eye. In fact, a smile can catch an eye in a blink.

The right smile is disarming and charming. It is a shield against the ills of the world. Backed up with love, a smile can help you conquer the world.

It's your secret weapon. Hone it to perfection.

Stand in the mirror and smile. Smile at yourself. Smile with love on your heart. Smile until you feel it and know it to be you.

Then go face the world.

You'll get all its treasure and enjoy it with pleasure.

Your smile is your greatest asset. Never leave home without it.

To quote little orphan Annie: "You're never fully dressed without a smile!"

Here's a smile boosting affirmation, "My smile is love and love is my smile. I am beautiful."

Day 7: Wake Up 20 Minutes Earlier

Today's task will take place at the end of the day. I know to most of us, sleep is a precious resource of which we never have enough. Health experts recommend 6-8 hours per night and that can really be a struggle for many of us with jobs, kids and chores around the house. With that said, having an extra 20 minutes in the morning can help knock out some of those dreaded chores, or at the very least, help to prevent you from rushing around in the morning trying to get out the door. This rush will inevitably kick off your day with a stress-filled anxiety attack. Starting your day in this manner can have halo effects on everything else you do that day and can prevent you from living your best life to the fullest potential.

I am not saying that setting your alarm 20 minutes earlier will not be a challenge; especially at first. This is one piece that will take some getting used to, but I promise, you will adapt and you will thank me later. I think you will find that it will take less time than you think to get your body acclimated and ready to roll on 20 minutes less sleep. If you're still struggling after a few days, there is always the option of going to bed 20 minutes earlier, which may happen naturally if you have less chores in the evening and are more relaxed.

Now that you have your alarm set 20 minutes earlier, the hard part starts. You actually have to WAKE UP AND GET OUT OF BED when the alarm goes off. You may need to try tricks like placing your alarm clock far away from the bed, so you have to actually get up to go and switch it off. REMOVE THE SNOOZE. I promise, you'll love it (although maybe not at first).

For me, getting up earlier has had many life-changing benefits. First, I've found that I really enjoy the quietness of my house. There is something very soothing about a dark and quiet house while I have my coffee. Also, it gives me time to do something that maybe I've been putting off. Sometimes, when I'm feeling really ambitious, I'll put on a YouTube video of a beginner's 20-minute yoga routine. I've discovered that it really gets my blood pumping while helping me calm down and relax all at the same time. Finally, as mentioned above, I feel less rushed when I get up a few minutes earlier, which sets the tone for a peaceful, positive and productive day.

So, go for it! Set that alarm! Get up early! And, start your day WINNING! I cannot wait to talk to you tomorrow.

Chapter 2: Second Phase

Day 8: Create a Budget that will Work for You

This is where so many people become confused and give up when they are trying to live on less, but it does not have to be difficult. You need to learn how to create a realistic budget and how to stick to it.

Budgets are easy, but sometimes when you have more going out than what is coming in, stress follows. For now, don't worry about balancing your budget, just worry about all of your main bills and your income.

Start by adding up all of the money you have coming into your home. If you have money coming in that is not guaranteed, such as child support, do not count this as your income. Only count what you know you will get no matter what. This is the amount on which you are going to base all of your spendings. The money that is not guaranteed can be considered a bonus, and we will discuss it later.

Next, add up all of the essential bills you have to pay. This means your electric, your phone, your internet, your cable, house payment and so forth. Do not count discretionary items, such as going out to eat, purchasing clothing and entertainment. Only list the living expenses that you have to pay.

Grab a notebook and use it specifically for budgeting your money. At the top of the page, you are going to write your income. Then create a column of bills and debts you need to pay such as house payment and electricity. Next to the bills, write down the amount that is paid. For bills such as your electricity, use an average payment. For example, my electric is higher in the winter but very low in the summer, by using an average I am able to leave some money in the bank in the summer to use for electric in the winter. (Tip: Many utility companies allow you to pay the average monthly.)

Add up the total of all of your bills and see how it compares to the amount of money you have coming in. If you don't have enough money coming in to cover what is going out, you will have to make some changes.

Finally, at the bottom of the page, you need to list additional items for which you typically need money, such as birthdays, school supplies, or clothing. These are items that may not come up every month but still need to be periodically covered.

Once you have this completed, you are ready to start looking at what can be cut from your budget so that you are able to live on less. But what are the benefits of being able to live on less? (Maybe the cable is not as important as you thought, especially if you are constantly stressing over not having enough money every month.)

I once saw a Facebook post that said, "We spend our entire life focusing on earning a living so that we can have a happy life, then we find out that we are so busy earning a living that we have no life to enjoy." Learning to live on less will ensure that you have time to actually enjoy life and not waste it working all the time.

Day 9: Take a Walk

Many health experts recommend at least 10,000 steps per day for a healthy lifestyle. I'm here to tell you that unless you are a server at a busy restaurant or a professional runner, getting 10,000 steps per day is HARD. I struggle to get them in on a daily basis, but when I do, I notice a difference in how I feel and in my energy levels. For me, walking has so many benefits that improve not only my physical health, but also my mental health.

First and foremost, walking gets the blood flowing. Taking a walk is exercise and it is essential for good cardiovascular health. Walking gives me a few minutes to escape and let my mind wander to things of interest to me and not just work or what my family should have for dinner that night. Sometimes, I just walk to clear my head, and getting moving allows me the opportunity to step away from it all, even if for only 15 minutes. In addition, I recommend trying to take your walk outside, if at all possible to breathe in the fresh air and soak up some vitamin D.

I know some of you are thinking that you would love to take walks, but you just don't have the time. Maybe you have meetings and conference calls all day and just don't have an extra 15-20 minutes to step away. Trust me I have days like these as well. In this situation, I like to schedule it so that I can take at least one of my calls on the move. I put on my earbuds with the built-in microphone and listen or talk while I walk. I've actually found that some of my best calls have come while I'm out on a walk, as exercise and physical activity have been proven to improve brain function. So, if you don't take a walk for yourself, take it for your company; they'll be glad you did. Get out there and get to stepping!

Day 10: Organize Your house

Hang a corkboard in your mudroom or foyer to help keep you organized as you dash out of the house. The board is perfect for those shopping lists, prescriptions, or reminder notes that you seem always to be forgetting. Give it some extra functionality by screwing a magnetic knife holder to the frame of your cork board. Use it to hold keys (not good for car keys with built-in chips), scissors, a screwdriver, and even a small flashlight.

Hang a large tote bag in a common area and use it to collect clothing and other items destined for donation.

Buy some clear plastic business card sheets to organize all those cards lying about. These sheets are also handy for organizing sewing kits, embroidery thread or even coupons. The larger divider sheets are perfect for storing recipes.

Between cell phones, MP3 players, PDA's, you name it, we have more devices charging than we have counter space. Organize your electronic chargers in one box with a hole in the bottom to insert a power bar cord. Attach the power bar to the bottom of the box and plug in all your electronic toys. Keep the lid open when in use to prevent heat build up.

Clothespins aren't just for hanging wet clothes. They make great closet organizers for hats, mitts and scarves. Glue the pins to the inside of closet doors and keep your mitts organized in the cold weather. Use the same idea in an office cupboard to hang memos, cards, photos or small calendars.

Use pretty glass knobs or other coordinating hardware to hang towels over the sink in the laundry room.

Sometimes candles will sit in a drawer for an entire year without being used, and they may easily be broken during that time. Next time you empty a roll of paper towels, use your empty cardboard roll to store candles, labeling each tube with the color and size of the candle.

The next time you have to go poking around a dark place like your crawl space or fuse box, have a flashlight ready to go. If your flashlight is metal, simply attach a small magnet to the outside of the fuse box, or glue a strip of Velcro for plastic versions. Do not forget to put batteries in the flashlight.

If you purchase large bags of dog food, simply empty into a small garbage pail for easy storage. Close the lid tightly and the food will stay fresh for weeks.

Organize the cupboard under the sink by hanging small items like scrubbers, rubber gloves and dust rags on clothespins or hooks found to the door's inside.

These are just some ideas, but the idea is to look around, embrace the clutter you see and do something about it!

Day 11: Pause and Give Thanks

Texts, emails and social media got us running. Bills, work and hustling for money got us running. Five minutes into the day and we are humming.

Life is a whirlwind moving along at the speed of light.

We got dreams. We got plans. We're building a better life.

That's good but we don't live in dreams. We can't experience the joy of life in plans. We can't build a better life without appreciating the life we're living now.

Pause for a moment and take a look at your surroundings. Stay at the moment.

Look at life.

Look for the good. Look for what's going right. See the blessings. Take it all in and give thanks.

Yes, things may not be as excellent as you would like. Give thanks for the good you see. Yes, many things may not be going exactly as you would like. Give thanks for what is turning in your favor. And yes, it's hard to bless the mess you may be experiencing. Do it anyway.

Reclaim your power. Show the world that society cannot bind you, technology cannot grind you, and fear cannot find you. Be the boss of you. Step out of the world.

Step into faith.

Focus your heart and mind on good and declare for yourself that everything – everything – is all right. Nothing has power over you.

Free yourself now, at this moment with this affirmation, "Everything is all right with me and my world. Only good happens to me. Everything is all right with me and my world. Only good happens to me. Everything is all right with me and my world.

Only good happens to me. Thank you. Thank you. Thank you, God."

Say it until you believe it. Believe it and you will see it. That's a promise.

Day 12: Ask for Help

If you are anything like me, then you have a problem admitting that you can't do it all. I really struggle with not having the answers or not being able to handle everything in my life, on my own. I'm the one who helps others, not the other way around. Well, I'm here to tell you two things:

1.   No one can do everything on their own and no one is an expert in all things.

2.   It's ok to seek help, guidance or advice from someone who is better than you at a task or an area of life.

Take an opportunity today to think of an area where you are not as strong as you would like to be. This could be any skill, including time management, money management, sales, writing, spreadsheets or something simple like doing a cart wheel. Find someone who is successful in an area where you could stand to improve and find out what they did to achieve this level of success. Tell them what you admire about them and seek their guidance. You would be surprised how many folks are willing to share their knowledge, especially when you stroke their ego a little.

If I could leave you with one key piece of advice from today's lesson it could be summed up in two words. Be vulnerable. It's ok to put yourself out there and admit you have weaknesses; because we all do. Weaknesses do not make you weak, but not admitting them will. Putting yourself out there and being vulnerable can be a key driver to success. It makes us uncomfortable, and stretches our boundaries, and ultimately teaches us something new.

Having trouble getting the conversation started? Try these icebreakers…

- "Hey there, can I get your advice on something?"
- "Can I pick your brain for a minute?"
- "Would you mind helping me with…?"

- "I've noticed you are amazing at _____. Do you have 30 minutes to show me a few tricks?"
- "I would love to be as good as you at _____. What's your secret?"

These are easy, to the point and difficult to say "no" to. Try it; the results will be phenomenal!

Day 13: Fill Your Heart with Love and Conquer Fear

Fear is the root of all anger, discord and conflict. Trace any negative action to its source and you will find fear.

Fear turns discussions into arguments, dislike into hatred and anger into murder. It can poison relationships and sabotage success. Unchecked fear will kill everything it touches – even you.

The first lesson a person learns when swimming is not to be afraid of the water. Fear causes panic. People who panic drown. The way to stop panicking and drowning is to calm down and float. The same is true when facing life's challenges.

When the arguing starts and you get a tightening in your belly, ask yourself what is it that we are talking about that makes me so afraid that now I am getting angry?

When the insult causes you to flinch and the anger swells, stop and reflect on the source. When the little pebble of dislike drops, before you say, "I don't like so-and-so," trace the reason to the root and you will find fear. You will also find fear at the root of a scary decision. Fear leads you to jump to conclusions and embrace bad decisions based on a boogey man shouting "what-ifs" at you.

Remember, fear causes panic. People who panic drown. Don't drown in the situation. Calm down and float. Shift your attention to love.

You may not feel the love in the heat of the moment. But if you are thinking love, you are not thinking about smacking someone upside their head. Even if all you can manage is to spell the word "L-O-V-E" in your mind, your brain is too busy to try to come up with the clever retort or insult in response. You are thinking love. You are calming down and floating.

You may not think love is the solution to a serious problem you are trying to solve or dilemma you are trying to unravel. Love will stop you from drowning in a pool of doubt as you flail about looking for an answer. Even if all you can manage at first is spelling the word love in your mind when you think of the challenge, this simple act will allow you to calm down and float. Eventually, you will make a better decision because you will be acting out of love instead of acting out of fear.

Love conquers fear. Put love in your heart now. When you draw on this love in a moment of battling fear, draw upon it as your armor against fear; the love you put there now will still be there, use it.

Here's a love centering affirmation, "This situation has no power over me. I am love. Love is me. I find the right and perfect solution in the right and perfect way to every challenge."

Day 14: Replace One Unhealthy Snack

For today's task, I want you to take one unhealthy snack and replace it with something nutritious. Perhaps, instead of potato chips, you make the move to carrots and hummus. Or, instead of a candy bar, you reach for an apple. You will be surprised how filling an apple can be. Not to mention, it is full of nutrients and is surprisingly sweet.

Trust me, I have been there. It is incredibly convenient AND delicious to grab that unhealthy snack and bypass the stuff that actually has nutritional value. But, if you can make that switch, you will end up taking in fewer calories while adding additional nutrients. These small but significantly better choices will lead to a healthier lifestyle, a better fitting wardrobe, and a better looking, more productive you. Go out there and eat well and look and feel great! Remember, one good choice leads to another.

Chapter 3: Third Phase

Day 15: Forgive

Life is a series of moments.

Moments make seconds. Seconds make minutes. Minutes make hours. Hours make days. Days make weeks. Weeks make months. Months make years. Years make a lifetime of living.

And in reality, that is how we live – moment to moment.

Every emotion we experience happens in the present. Even if we are giggling about a memory or fretting about the future, we don't experience either outside of right when we are thinking in the present moment. We are living right now with our feelings – good or bad, happy or sad. And we take them with us from one moment to the next.

But it all starts with the moment we are living right now – this second.

Not convinced? Stop breathing and see if the memory of breathing yesterday comforts you. No one suffocating cares about how they might breathe tomorrow. All they want is to breathe now – at the moment they are experiencing.

Thankfully most of us don't have to suffocate to get focused on the moment.

The question is, now that you know how important this moment is as a building block of your life, how are you living it? Are you dragging anger and resentment from this one to the next? Are you unwilling to forgive even the simplest slight or harshest transgression at this moment?

Remember moments make seconds that turn quickly into a lifetime of living. Use this moment wisely. Forgive someone. Even if you can only manage to forgive for a second, do it. Keep at it and you will find you have built a lifetime of living in forgiveness. And that's a good thing.

Here's a tool to help. Take a deep relaxing breath and say, "I am a forgiving person. There is only love in me and my life."

Day 16: Be Hopeful

Become a prisoner of hope.

Don't weigh the odds and then make a decision to be optimistic. Don't try to calculate all the variables. Don't try to envision every possible outcome.

The universe is too big. The variables are too fluid. There's no way to wrap the mind around all the possible outcomes in an infinite universe.

Pride comes before the fall. Recognize pride's arrogance in choosing to be optimistic based on running the numbers. Avoid the fall.

Avoid the fall by not becoming a prisoner of a formula concocted to navigate life. Weighing the odds as a path to optimism fails. Pessimism is always there, lurking in the background. Whatever positive outcome may be yielded from running the numbers draws its inverse as well. Fear stalks success from the shadows of doubt.

Cast aside the shadows. Stand firm in the light inside the cheerful walls of hope. With hope, there are no calculations, no variables to weigh and no negatives to compare.

Hope defies the odds. Faith sees through circumstances. Together, they achieve the impossible and take us where logic will fail us.

Ironically, when we are faced with the darkest times, we often become a prisoner of hope and chain ourselves to faith by default. They are our last resorts when everything else fails us. We surrender and in doing so, achieve what we thought was impossible.

Stop doing the math. Erase the formula. Become a prisoner of hope now, in this moment.

Use this affirmation, "I believe in good. I see the good. I experience good. I know all good is happening for me now."

Day 17: Communicate Effectively

Have you ever come across a situation where someone is on the losing end just because of his/her lack of effective communication? Well, I have plenty of experiences to elaborate on this phenomenon. Have any of following instances happened with you?

You thought your boss would love your idea, but she did not give it serious consideration because you were not able to make her understand exactly what you meant. You thought your spouse wanted you to praise him/her and indeed you wanted to, but you failed to convey the praise. You did not get a job, although you were the most eligible candidate, because you could not successfully convince the hiring manager to understand your qualifications.

Every once in a while, I used to find myself in one of these types of situations. I then decided to strategize and determine if I could improve my position in these situations by enhancing my communication skills, and trust me, I thank God for that day when He made me move in this direction. We can all continuously improve our communication techniques. Even though you think you are perfect at communicating, you will soon realize that much room for improvement exists once you start working on it. Several rules to the game of communication are key components that you need to keep in mind if you want the receiver of your communications to not just hear you, but *listen* to you:

1. The receiver is the king of the game, regardless of who you are and who the receiver is, hopefully the receiver is also a *listener*, because any kind of communication is effective only if it is two-way i.e., the person with whom you want to communicate is actually listening. So, forget that you are the boss, forget that you are the elder, forget everything and mold yourself to suit the receiver of the communication.

2. Do not be too specific or too detailed while communicating (except for SMS, which should be short enough).

3. Keep it simple. Do not complicate your language. Complicated language will not do any good except for impressing or tiring the listener and making them think that he/she need not listen as he/she will not understand it anyway. It's okay to use jargon sometimes, but do not make it a habit or overuse such terms, at least not in very important communications.

4. Clarity of thoughts is an extremely important tool for effective communication as you can only convey something that you understand yourself. Understanding something yourself does not ensure that you will communicate it well, however, so be careful to break it down into manageable nuggets of information.

5. Be confident of your position. First, you need to believe something completely, to make others believe it.

6. Watch your wording. Sometimes, you may tend to use words that you do not really want to use, and in fact you do not even know how they will impact the listener. Be careful and keep watch over your own vocabulary, and avoid talking without thinking at all. Use a filter before speaking. Some filters may be: Is this true? Is this relevant? Is this hurtful? Is this biased? Do I want someone to repeat this and quote me? Try to be politically correct at least in public places, if not with family.

I hope you seriously consider adopting these techniques. Enjoy your day.

Day 18: Calm Your Mind

Calm your mind at this moment. It's really not that big of a challenge. Nothing is that challenging because nothing is permanent. Nothing lasts forever. Not one physical item. Your car, house, the street on which you live, and the city in which you live can fall away without a moment's notice.

Nothing is permanent. Every tree, every bird, every rock, every drop of water evaporates into the nothingness from whence it came. Even your body will return to its origins and break down into the very molecules and atoms that make the universe.

Ashes to ashes and dust to dust are not an end, but another step on a journey everything and everyone will take.

That's the challenge. We temporarily mitigate the challenge by preserving museum artifacts and by keeping bodies functioning longer with medical advances. We write our thoughts on paper, in books, on computer chips, and in the vast cloud of technology. Eventually, they will all go the way of dust.

The only big challenge about anything is the importance we give it in our own minds. The universe doesn't care. Even stars eventually grow cold and wink out of existence. What chance does your favorite chair have against that? No chance at all.

This is not to say we shouldn't try. We should try because life is worth living. It's just that when we can accept the impermanence of everything in the universe, we gain perspective.

Perspective saves us from the disaster of thinking and acting as if what we're doing, or wanting or holding onto are the most important things in the universe. Stars eventually grow cold and wink out of existence. What chance does your coveted item, your brilliant scheme, your careful planning have against that? No chance at all.

Keep everything in perspective. Mt. Everest is but a speck from space. A diamond is still a rock. One man's treasure is another man's trash. There's always a bigger fish to catch.

Calm your mind at this moment. It's not that big of a challenge.

Free yourself from fear with perspective. Appreciate and give thanks for the people and things you have now – today.

Take deep, relaxing breaths with this affirmation, "I live in the moment with everything and everyone. I accept all my good and give thanks for what is now."

Day 19: Reduce Sugar Intake

You are getting so close; congratulations! Take a moment and celebrate your success today! You have come extremely far and are right on the cusp of completing this program and jump-starting your new and improved life. Let's finish strong!

Today, we are going to replace one sugary drink with a tall, cool glass of water. Our bodies are made up primarily of water and we need to continuously pump more and more in to replace what we lose in sweat. Your body needs optimal amounts of water to function at max capacity and keep you running strong and smooth all day long. Try and find an area where you can make this essential swap that will offer multiple benefits to your health and to your life.

Do you drink sugary sodas, flavored coffees, iced mochas, even diet sodas loaded with artificial sugars? If so, these are what we are looking to replace. Don't worry, I am not asking you to go cold turkey and give them up all together. Start by replacing just one and work your way up from there.

By making the switch to water you will feel full, causing you to eat less. You will feel more hydrated which has benefits for your mental alertness and skin tone. You will be sheltered from the typical crash that comes along with a burst of sugar, helping you to be more productive throughout the day. Plus, you will save the calories, helping you to lose weight and look and feel better. Now, who doesn't want that?

Day 20: Relax and Let Good Things Happen

Be encouraged. There are seven billion people in the world. All of them are moving through life just like you. They stumble. They fall. They get up and keep moving.

They move through the bad and get to the good. They move through the good and get to the bad. Then they move through the worst, and eventually get to the good stuff again.

And so it goes, on and on…

Like mice constantly searching for cheese, people live life running back and forth between good and bad, ultimately hunting for something better. They are anxious and fearful even in good times because the next bad thing is right around the corner. When the bad times come they are anxious and fearful because, well…things are bad. How else are you supposed to feel?

Good to bad, bad to good, good to bad, bad to good, and back again. The whole thing is crazily exhausting. Honestly running back and forth between the two extremes should drive a person insane – because it is crazy to run in circles all the time.

That's the world – crazy. And the world expects you to be crazy right along with it. Stop running around like a crazy person!

Be encouraged. Good things are happening. Relax and let them happen to you. Notice the good in you and your life. Even when things seem bad, even when things are legitimately bad, good is still there – right where you are at the moment.

Pay attention to the good. Give thanks for the good. If all you have is one slice of bread, eat it with a grateful heart. If you have two slices of bread with your favorite meat, lettuce and tomatoes, but no mayo, eat the sandwich and be grateful. You don't have to starve to learn how to take what you have and be grateful because it beats being hungry.

This is not a lesson about settling for less. Far from it, this is a lesson about getting more. Recognize what is truly good by being grateful for what sustains you and keeps you alive. The rest is extra stuff that's nice to have, but won't kill you if you don't. Rise above crazy and know goodness.

Congratulations on all of your progress throughout this journey and I hope you continue moving forward in a positive direction. See you tomorrow for the final day of our 21-day challenge.

Here's an affirmation, "I am in the flow of good because good is always happening. I relax and let it happen to me. Thank you. Thank you."

Day 21: Review Your Previous Habits and Set New Goals

Give yourself a massive pat on the back for making it through this 21 Day exercise! All of these changes were small in nature, but I am hoping that you truly saw massive gains in your life. And, I hope it does not stop here. I hope you continue to put into practice the techniques we went through together to ensure exponential growth in your personal and professional lives. On our final day together, I want you to review and work on new goals.

Do you remember those goals you wrote out in Chapter 1 on the very first day of reading this book? I want you to dig those out and re-read them now. Really spend some time walking through them and thinking about them. Now, spend a few minutes answering the following questions about those goals:

- Did you achieve any of the goals you set on day 1?

- Were there any goals that you did not achieve, but you came really close to achieving?

- How have your goals changed since you started this book?

    ❖ Are your goals more singular, more focused or broader?

    ❖ Have your priorities and goals shifted in any way?

    ❖ Did some goals seem daunting in the beginning, but now seem too easy?

After this review, I am sure some of you have already started working on new goals; or, at least making adjustments to your existing goals. Get creative with them, and have a little fun letting your imagination wander. Best of luck and keep driving forward!

Conclusion

So where can you go from here? You've learned a lot about what makes habits form, and how to tell a good habit from a bad one. You've even learned how to replace your bad habits with good ones, and how to make them work for you. You know how to start changing your life, and you've even been given a 21-day habit-changing challenge to help you get started. With all of this excellent information, you're ready to get out there and make a difference in your life, one habit at a time.

So, what are you waiting for? You've got what you need to get started. All you have to do now is pick a bad habit you want to change or choose a good habit you want to start, and work through the 21-day challenge. In no time, you'll see differences in your work, your home life, and your overall emotional well-being.

You owe it to yourself to practice good habits!

-- Anne Gilmore

Made in the USA
San Bernardino, CA
09 August 2019